Thank ~

Colin McAllister

2 May 2018

Can I Scan?

– COLIN MCALLISTER –

An environmentally friendly book printed and bound in England by
www.printondemand-worldwide.com

www.fast-print.net/store.php

Can I Scan?
Copyright © Colin McAllister 2012

ISBN 978-178035-493-4

First published 2012 by
FASTPRINT PUBLISHING
Peterborough, England.
Printed by Printondemand-Worldwide

Contents

1

Religious

Sonnet
The St Andrews Botanic Garden

I'll say the St Andrews Garden Botanic
In scale is positively titanic;
With flowers and trees from parts exotic,
It pleases the eye in ways quite hypnotic!

A mere fifty years in the Canongate,
It looks like it has a much older date.
Edinburgh has its gardens Arboretum,
But St Andrews equals or even beats 'em!

All credit must go to the gardens' staff,
Who work and do not do anything by half,
Resulting in a visual treasure
For St Andrews that is beyond measure.

If to this garden you have not yet been,
I urge you not to miss this lovely scene!

Sonnet
The St Andrews Local Plan

Fife Council planners want houses to build
On fertile fields that Fife farmers have tilled.
Northbank Farm, which has heard the plump of hooves
Will be covered by a rats' run of roofs.
The Uni wants science and business parks
On land that has heard the singing of the larks.
Let all citizens rise up as one man
And reject the St Andrews Local Plan!

TINA – there is no alternative –
Is an argument with more holes than a sieve.
Let not these men despoil our western ridge,
Let the Uni build its parks in Guardbridge!
Guardbridge, which has lost jobs from its paper mill,
Would welcome the Uni's parks with a will!
Let all citizens rise up as a man
And reject the St Andrews Local Plan!

St Andrews citizens, if you love your toon,
Don't let the council planners ding it doon!

HMO★

Tune: Tannenbaum

O HMO! O HMO!
How much I'd like to see you go!
Fife Council has been far too lax,
Students should pay the Council Tax!

Each new HMO makes me frown,
They rip the heart out of the town.
To absentee landlords I say:
"We don't want you, so go away!"

Now, Fife Council, please get a grip
And admit you have made a slip.
We St Andreans love our town
These HMOs will ding it down!

★ House in Multiple Occupation

Sonnet
The Grim Wolf

St Andrews once was a wondrous place,
But the grim wolf yearly grows apace.
When St Andreans awoke from their sleep,
They found they'd been cleared – for student sheep!

The proliferation of HMOs
Has been the cause of the townees' woes.
Since students don't pay the Council Tax,
This really gets up the locals' backs!

Not affording to live in their own old town,
Locals must give way to the student gown,
And one result of this sticky wicket
Is that they forfeit their Links golf ticket!

The grim wolf's motto is "Strive to be the best" -
Today this means, "We come first and forget the rest!"

Sonnet
Scottish Celibates

These humble lines I wish to dedicate
To each and ev'ry Scots male celibate.
I don't mean those who are without a flame,
But non-players of the Royal and Ancient game.

How do you spend Saturday afternoons?
Is it by reading soppy Mills and Boons?
The birdies you can see on golfing greens
Are far better than on your TV screens!

The fairer sex I by no means despise,
But golf for me is a far greater prize.
If you miss a putt, does your ball cry, "Fool!"
Or, after a poor shot, "Go back to school!"

Men can be with women or be without,
But without golf? Never, there is no doubt!

Sonnet
Slow Play

Now we are in the merry month of May,
We are once again subject to slow play.
Visiting golfers and caddies abound,
And it takes longer to complete a round.
This is what to the ranger I always say:
"Move them along, move them along, JJ!"

Four and a half hours to play a round
Is not exactly the speed of sound!
To those who play at the speed of a snail,
I say: "Go and play elsewhere – go to Crail!"
This is what to the ranger I always say:
"Move them along, move them along, JJ!"

If only all rangers were like JJ,
We'd not be under the curse of slow play!

Sonnet

The Castle Course

Shall I compare you to Kingsbarns Golf Course?
It is more scenic and more playable.
Kingsbarns is a links that I do endorse,
Better designed and more enjoyable!

The Castle's greens have some crazy borrows,
That will throw a well-hit shot off the line,
Yielding fewer joys than golfing sorrows.
This is not what I'd call good course design!

Kingsbarns has the look of authentic links,
The Castle's synthetic, fake and unreal.
Kingsbarns can be sometimes a teasing minx,
But the Castle quite fails my heart to steal!

Elephant and Castle's a better name
For the graveyard of some really big game!

Noordwijk Golf Club

By the sea is the golf course of Noordwijk,
And quite near there runs many a Dutch dyke.
Sand dunes and trees adorn every view,
But of bunkers, there are only a few.

Best of all, are the members and staff
With whom I've had many a laugh.
It seems that half of them had worked for Shell,
Which must be why the club is run so well.

No need for a lighthouse – Natali's smile
Can light up the scene for many a mile.
The lady starter is also a star,
Welcoming golfers from near and far.

Wim, my host, Quik by name and quick by swing,
He and his wife Corrie, are just the thing.
Just Kerkoff who gives the ball such a strike
Can hit fairways no wider than a dyke.

So thanks to Wim, Corrie, Just and Annette,
Your hospitality I shall never forget.
I hope that you'll come and visit my hame
And enjoy, with me, many a golf game.

Sonnet
To Peter Alliss

The Voice of Golf, that is Peter Alliss,
Gentle in tone, exudes both joy and bliss.
When a professional misses a putt,
All you'll hear from him is a mild tut-tut!

Peter is the master of the quick ad lib,
Always well-informed, and this is no fib!
When a golfer's putt stopped right on the lip,
The pain he'd soothe with some clever quip.

His secret is that he has been there before;
That is why he is not a crashing bore!
If nothing is happening, he'll give a quote
Or fill the time with some old anecdote!

Well done Peter, you're in the Hall of Fame!
Without you, golf would never be the same!

The Credit Lunch

I'd like to offer you a tasty lunch;
How about a bar of our Credit Crunch?
Today we have Credit Default Swaps –
Far more flavoured than any lollipops!

We also have some Options on Call –
You'll make money if the price does not fall!
Or, if these do not your preference suit,
We can also serve Options to Put.

Why purchase wholemeal biscuits digestive,
When you could buy a Credit Derivative?
Why acquire shares for a pot of honey?
Buy instead Options for lots less money!

Try one of our best recommendations –
Collateralised Debt Obligations!
Through the means of securitisation,
We pass on the risk of debt derogation.

I'll let you into my inner circuit –
Just invest in my off balance sheet Conduit!
If you engage in plenty of gearing,
You can get huge returns with no fearing!

If you are in a financial pickle,
Then try our Structured Investment Vehicle!
Don't make soup out of old chicken bones,
But use instead some of our ninja loans!

If you wish to invest hard-earned wages,
Why not try one of our subprime mortgages?
Don't believe that talk of credit bubble,
Those who speak that way are only trouble!

If you've cash, and don't know where to park it,
Why not invest it in the stock market?
Those who say it is like playing poker,
Haven't met an honest stockbroker!

What I earn is my bid to offer spread,
I trade on margin, without any dread.
I'm not driven either by fear of greed,
I trade only my family to feed!

If you ever have a toxic asset
Have no fear – to someone else just pass it.
Just make sure that when the music has stopped,
From your books it has been well and truly dropped!

Remember when you come to pay the bill,
Only with cash, we'll let you ring our till.
Now that you have had your great credit fling,
What it comes down to is that cash is king!

The moral of this tale is clear,
Even if at first it does not appear.
All will know by the end of the credit crunch.
That there is no such thing as a free lunch!

Sonnet
Alice In Euroland

There are four countries that are called the PIGS,⋆
Replete with sunshine, olives, wine and figs.
All four are in economic distress,
So how did they get into this mess?

These countries that are on the southern fringe
All went on a fiscal policy binge,
As in euros they could easily borrow
Without giving any thought to tomorrow.

The Euro's monetary straitjacket
In the end will cost them quite a packet.
If they could let their currencies float,
They'd not need help from the Euro-lifeboat.

Countries that don't play the monetary fool
Are wise to remember the Tinbergen Rule!⋆⋆

⋆PIGS – Portugal, Italy, Greece and Spain
⋆⋆ Tinbergen Rule states that the number of independent policy
instruments must equal the number of independent policy
targets.
Policy instruments are fiscal policy, monetary policy, supply side
policies, welfare policies and exchange rate policies.
Policy targets are full employment, stable prices, economic
growth, greater equality in the distribution of income and wealth,
and balance of payments equilibrium.

Timeo Danaos Et Dona Quaerentes
(I fear the Greeks even when asking for gifts)

The Eurozone crisis, in which we are,
Has its root in Greece, a country too far.
An economic dread now chills my bones;
I fear the Greeks when asking for loans.

If the Greeks default on their euro debt,
A great tsunami will Europe beset,
Drowning many of its banks with deadly losses,
A fall like that of Rhodes's Colossus.

Northern Europe shies at paying the Greek bill,
But if they will not pay it, then who will?
So it looks as if there is no way but
For the banks to take a Grecian haircut.

It follows investors bank shares will shun
And the banks themselves may face a run,
Unless their statesmen erect a sea wall
Of high finance, this ruin to forestall.

If there is no such monetary boost,
The Euro's chickens will come home to roost.
An economic dread now chills my bones,
I fear the Greeks when asking for loans.

The European economic hubris
Thought the euro would be a source of bliss.
Here I offer you my catechesis
And, "There's no free lunch", my exegesis.

Sonnet

Italian Vespers

Signor Silvio Berlusconi
Struts about like a macaroni,
But Italy now tires of this pasta
And so the Quirinal's word is "Basta!"

Italy's debt is too great to swallow,
So, for Silvio, now there's no tomorrow!
Blood-letting there will be in the Forum
Before Rome restores fiscal decorum.

Politicians supply-side reforms must pass
To escape from this financial impasse.
If by Rome these changes are rejected
Then from the Euro, they'll be ejected.

What the future holds, I have no idea,
But, for Rome, "finita la commedia!"

Sonnet
Down The Liffey

When the Irish switched to Euros from the Punt,
They thought that they had pulled off quite a stunt!
But the project turned out rather iffy,
As the Irish banks went down the Liffey.

Low interest rates fed a building boom,
So housing prices to the skies did zoom,
But when suddenly boom turned into bust,
The Irish economy bit the dust.

Then the Irish grasped the financial nettle
And soon they were back in finer fettle.
The Euro crisis was quite a shock,
But there is life yet in the old shamrock!

Very soon there will be a new Irish dawn
And a smile again on the leprechaun!

Sonnet
Chancellor Merkel

Chancellor Merkel, who loves to say "Nein",
Abhors the Mediterranean whine;
With her French pal, Nicolas Sarkozy,
She holds summits that are frank but cosy.

When the Greeks and Italians ask for cash,
She says, "Your economies have turned to ash.
If only you'd worked and saved much harder.
You wouldn't have such an empty larder."

"The solution is for you to reform,
Only this way you'll escape the storm.
Instead of asking me for a loan,
What you need is some Teutonic backbone!"

"We Germans have suffered hyperinflation,
So we don't want it now in this generation."

Sonnet
The Eurozone Crisis

The French and the Germans have a plan grand
To repeal the laws of supply and demand.
Why should world bond markets hold them in sway?
Capital markets rule – it is just not okay!

The Chinese Government has a great wheeze,
Which allows them to sell their debt with much ease.
Their banks' assets must be held in yuan,
All foreign holdings are under the ban.

Now if Europe had a Politburo,
This could be the saving of the Euro.
As banks would have to buy government debt,
Budget deficits wouldn't give cause to fret.

But the lesson of the sovereign debt crunch
Is, "There is no such thing as a free lunch!"

Sonnet
Quantitative Easing

When the economy is near freezing,
Then it is time for some quantitative easing.
When the outlook is far from sunny,
Then it is time to print some more money.

The only trouble with this sort of thing
Is that you cannot push a piece of string.
More money won't rescue us from the brink,
If it goes down an economic sink.

Money's no use if people won't spend it.
It's no use if banks won't lend it.
We need to follow a different track
To get the economy off the rack.

Investing in new infrastructure
Might just heal the economic rupture.

Sonnet
The Ideas Factory

Deep in the volcano that is the brain
Is a team working with all might and main,
Forging ideas like well-tempered steel,
Until in words, the thoughts do congeal.

Poems are but one-tenth inspiration,
Whilst the rest is nine-tenths perspiration.
As surfacing lava flows when it erupts,
So the unconscious, the conscious disrupts.

The brain is the city that never sleeps
With thoughts like whales swimming in its great deeps.
Then, like a whale which is beached on the shore,
There comes a thought which was not there before.

O how marvellous is the human brain!
Praise be to Him, by Whom it was designed!

Sonnet
Adam And Eve

Adam was a bored and lonely young man,
As all around the world his eyes did scan
But found nothing his boredom to relieve,
Till God sent a helpmate, whose name was Eve.

Now in Eden's garden was laughter heard,
But Eve always had to have the last word.
Yet the pair were happy for quite a while,
Till Eve was tempted by the serpent's guile.

Then Eve some of the fateful apple ate –
Why didn't she just try a luscious date?
So from the garden they were both thrown out
And their trust was replaced by mutual doubt.

The moral of this story is quite clear –
What you wish for may come, a little dear!

Sonnet
Christmas 2009

As I head back homewards to the east,
I want to thank you for your Christmas feast,
Where smiles and friendship are all around
And children's laughter does abound.

Nowhere more welcome have I felt
Than in the homely House of Belt,
Where mixed with all the Christmas cheer
Is lots of good food, wine and beer.

So my thanks to both of you, Ed and Em,
With you there is no "Us" and "Them",
For all are made most welcome in your house,
Be they stranger, friend or daughter's spouse.

So I wish to all of you, far and near,
A Happy Christmas and a Good New Year!

E-Mail

I'd like to say a word about e-mail,
It's a sort of electric blackmail.
I do not wish to go that kind of walk,
For me it's always better to talk.

Today this may put me beyond the pale,
My letters having the speed of a snail,
Yet if my news arrives quite unhurried,
With viruses I'm not at all worried.

I'm not trapped in some electronic jail,
Pressed to reply at once and without fail.
I can reply to letters at my ease,
The tyrant computer, I need not please.

The computer's demands need not prevail,
Nor do its spam messages me assail.
Instead I've time to reply with measure,
Answering letters can then be a pleasure.

The dearth of good letters makes me bewail,
Text messages it seems now do prevail.
Soon we will have lost the power of speech,
Civilised talk will be beyond our reach.

Something in our society does fail,
When our life leaves but an electronic trail.
What I bemoan is the loss of our space,
Life is now lived at too fast a pace.

So what is the moral of this little tale?
Can we not halt this electric gale
And make a return to more leisured times,
Something that with our nature better chimes?

Stovies

Haggis may well be Scotland's national dish,
But a plate of stovies is all I wish!
Reamin', reekin', tasty in ev'ry way,
What better meal for a wintry day?

Pommes étouffées is what the French would say,
Mince, onions and tatties, give me I pray!
Stovies are the food that Scots bairns do crave,
Stovies are what has made Scotland the Brave!

Wind Turbines

O wind turbine, O wind turbine,
Your silhouette is so divine!
Donald Trump is in such a rage
Because his golf course you upstage!

You're useless as a source of power,
As the wind blows not every hour,
But you will have been worth your pay
If Donald Trump you've sent away!

Now wind power is the biggest scam,
Its greenery is but a sham!
Scotland's landscape it does despoil,
We're better far with North Sea oil!

On tidal power we can rely,
It is by far the better buy!
Scotland's coasts have many a firth,
Let's use their tides for all our worth!

Lament For Mary, Queen Of Scots

Child of James the Fifth and Mary of Guise,
Tall and stately, well the eye you did please!
Fairest of all the princesses of France,
You excelled in every courtly dance.

When Francis the Second died by ill chance,
You had to leave your beloved France
To take up your throne in a land of tumult
And suffer John Knox's scorn and insult.

When the death of Darnley at Kirk o' Field
Was blamed on you, then your fate was sealed,
Impasse with the Lords at Carberry Hill,
Next confinement in Loch Leven's castle still.

Escape from prison, then defeat at Langside
Meant in Scotland there was nowhere to hide,
So then you fled from the land of your birth
To England, and across the Solway Firth.

Held captive in England for twenty years,
Then put on trial by hand-picked English peers,
The evidence of the Casket Letters
Was forged like the iron of prison fetters.

Having spent time in the prisoner's dock,
You were condemned to die on the axeman's block.
O Marie Stuart, you led a tragic life,
Queen of France, of Scots, mother and wife!

Scion of more than one hundred Scots Kings,
My respectful homage this paean brings!
You were more sinned against than sinning,
Yes, in your end was your beginning!

To A Leech

Halt! Where are you going, blood-sucking worm?
Your impudence's enough to make me squirm.
How well you have used your office's term
        To bloat yourself!
You act as if it were your private firm
        To make your pelf.

You selfish, scheming, swollen figure,
Always ettling to make your pay bigger,
Looking down on others with a snigger
        From such a height!
Your arrogance will be your gravedigger,
        You'll get a fright!

You crawl up the body corporate
Your bloodlust with cash and power you sate,
Your career is like a burn in spate,
        You're not swerved!
And a rich retirement you await,
        So well deserved!

But soon the public will awaken
And then your hubris will be shaken.
The people will demand your bacon,
        Then you'll squeal!
When from you your office will be taken,
        You'll come to heel!

Envoi

O wad some Power the giftie gi'e us
To see oursel's as ithers see us!
It wad frae monie a blunder free us,
      An foolish notion:
What airs in dress an' gait wad lea'e us,
      An ev'n devotion!

(From *To a Louse* by Robert Burns)

Nomads Of The Wind
November 2010

It was in November 2010
That I ventured from my Scottish den
To cruise the Pacific Ocean
For two weeks of perpetual motion.

Our leader was Geraldine, or JD,
Tall, and bright-eyed, and slender was she.
"Good morning, good morning!" – all was said twice –
Always ready with hints and good advice

Then there was Brad, who'd been in Vietnam,
A man not backward in downing a dram!
"Scruffy passengers, so unlike a Marine!
Clipper Odyssey's keel, I'll have them careen!"

Pam Le Noury knows more things about fish
Than you could dare ask, or ever could wish!
Her accent is nasal, and just a bit posh!
It's by teaching snorkelling she earns her dosh.

Louis Justin speaks with quite a French lilt
On latitude, longitude and the Earth's tilt
And knows about things that are as cryptic
As the obliquity of the ecliptic!

It's from Vancouver that Colin Baird hails,
There's nothing he doesn't know about whales!
At home you'll see him in a Pontiac,
At sea what he drives is a Zodiac!

There was another Zodiac driver
Cobus by name, and he was no skiver!
He'd expertly steer you safe from the rocks,
This fervent follower of the Springboks!

Then there was Guy, who came from the Seychelles,
About which, many a story he'd tell.
He'll speak for hours of his love of Aldabra!
To stop him you must say "Abracadabra!"

Michael Moore is from the United States
But is not quite as geeky as Bill Gates!
There isn't a place he hasn't been –
It's our good luck that he is on our scene!

Another staff member was Simon Boyes,
Who knows about birds and all their ploys.
He spoke about the booby with red feet
And how the frigate bird did it cheat.

Also on board was the renowned Sue Flood,
Nature photography is in her blood!
She has worked on "The Planet Earth"
And filmed animals when giving birth.

Then there is the Captain, and his motley crew.
They're from many countries, and not a few.
There's nothing for them that's too much trouble.
As we sail around in our South Seas bubble!

The last word must be about me and you,
Together we have been in places new,
And as we go on our different ways,
I hope you'll think that those were happy days!

Sonnet
What Is Love?

What is love? Is it just an emotion,
Or is it only the heart's commotion?
Some say it is a sickness of the heart
Or a wound inflicted by Cupid's dart.

Is love just a mere infatuation,
Product of a passing situation,
Or is love the giving of one's heart
And also the pain of being apart?

Love is wanting the best for the other
Love is the self-giving of a mother.
Love is the bond between a husband and wife
And their love is what gives the world new life.

What is love? It is a constant forgiving.
What is love? It's our reason for living!

Sonnet
On Turning Seventy

I have now reached the age of seventy,
Which sounds worse than ten, and three times twenty!
Why do we care about certain numbers,
So much that it keeps us from our slumbers?

Yet I confess I've reached that certain stage
When I can no longer ignore my age.
There is no doubt that my fuller figure
Is accompanied by lesser vigour.

All I do now is mere window-shopping
At passing girls, without stopping.
But at a distance I still can admire,
With no involvement in love's deep quagmire!

So there is no point in useless fretting,
My problems I solve by just forgetting!

Sonnet

The Prison Of Loneliness

Are you in a prison of loneliness?
Suffering is our path to holiness.
Be consoled, your sorrows on this earth,
Borne with patience, in Heav'n are of great worth!

You long for day and then you long for night,
But most of all, you long for some respite.
Just as winter's starkness gives way to spring,
Then have faith that this year, new hope will bring.

Most of all, know that you are not alone!
There's One True Friend who will not you disown!
He is there with you in your utmost plight
And will shepherd you through the darkest night.

So lift up your heart and be of good cheer,
Renew your life, and cast away your fear!

Sonnet
Depression

"O God, I could be bounded in a nutshell, and count myself a king of infinite space, were it not that I have bad dreams"
                                        - Hamlet

Depression is a sort of mental death,
As if the mind had drawn its last breath
And drifted down dark corridors quite blind,
And to the loss of light had been consigned.

And in that deep darkness no dog does bark
Nor is ever heard the song of a lark,
Nor in that empty silence forlorn
Does there seem to be any glint of dawn.

But a time comes when black turns into white
And the sunrise of hope dispels the night,
And the mind is released from its dark cell,
And once again it knows that all is well.

So if you are still in that prison drear,
Be sure your dawn will come, and have no fear.

Sonnet
The Owl Of Wisdom

The average owl does not say that much,
But what it does sounds just like double-Dutch!
Inscrutable of face, its thoughts beyond reach,
The answer it gives is one almighty screech!

People of many words think they know it all,
But perhaps they are riding for a fall!
When one's mouth is open, it's hard to learn,
But silence gives time the truth to discern.

Watch and weigh your words, as if they were pearls!
Do not throw them about in wasteful whirls!
Words are like bullets – make them hit the mark!
This is the way to be the brightest spark!

You see those Trappist monks wearing their cowls?
In their silence they're far wiser than owls!

Sonnet
Clifford And Mina Mckee

It is sixty years that you've been married!
They've not been hurried, they've not been harried,
And that young lad that once was so bold
Has grown slowly and gracefully old,
And that young lassie that you thought such a catch
Has proved for you the perfect match.

I've met you in the autumn of your years
And I sense that for you, life has no fears.
I'm sure those years have gone by in a flash –
Memories are worth more than lots of cash!
Who knows how many more years are in store?
At any rate, I wish you many more.

Now that we've come to the parting of our ways,
I wish you joy for the rest of your days.

The Causeway Coast

I'll sing the praises of the Causeway Coast
Which must be Northern Ireland's greatest boast!
Between the cliffs of this basaltic land
Are scattered beaches of golden sand.

From Port Ballantrae to Ballycastle
You can travel without any hassle,
And if it is whiskey that gives you thrills,
Then stop to take a dram of Old Bushmills!

Also if golf is the name of your game,
Then Royal Portrush has the greatest fame,
But don't miss Portstewart and Castlerock!
They are fine courses, of which you should take stock.

I should also mention the Harbour Bar –
It is Northern Ireland's finest by far!
Don Giovanni's is a great place to eat,
If Italian food is your kind of treat.

Another place that for me is a star
Is the one and only Ramore Wine Bar.
Its roast duck and orange sauce is so good,
I'd have it every day if I could!

In Portrush I've passed many happy days,
Though mostly hidden from the sun's rays,
But the people's welcome is of the best
So my encomium there I will rest.

From Amsterdam To The Black Sea

Amsterdam was my birth canal
For a journey that was never banal.
Our cruise on the Rhine brought us to Cologne.
It has a great cathedral, I must own.

World War II left Koblenz mostly a wreck.
The Mosel meets the Rhine at Deutsches Eck,
Then through the Rhine Gorge past Lorelei Rock
To Rüdesheim, home of many a good hock.

From Mainz to Heidelberg on the Neckar,
(Thank goodness Allied bombs did not wreck her),
Then Miltenberg and Wertheim on the Main,
Pretty places with plenty of good wine.

Würzburg, wine capital of Franconia
Is decked with all colours of begonia!
At Bamberg you can try their smoked beer.
I don't recommend it, it's rather queer!

To Nuremberg, home of Albrecht Dürer,
And also the rally grounds of Der Führer.
Then on to Regensberg or Ratisbon;
Its mediaeval glories are not all gone.

An extra day there we had to stay
As low water levels blocked our way.
So to Liberation Hall on Michelsberg
And the baroque abbey of Weltenburg.

Back on course next day we arrived at Passau,
Where the Inn and Ilz rivers join the Donau.
Next day we sailed through the valley Wachau,
'Neath Melk Abbey's cliff we anchored our prow.

Then Dürnstein Castle, gaol of Richard the First,
Before a wine-tasting which quenched not our thirst.
In Vienna we did the tourist run
And after noon some went to the Schönbrunn.

On Sunday we reached Bratislava's city,
Slovakia's capital, and so pretty.
Late that night we reached floodlit Budapest,
In good time for next day's St Stephen's fest.

We then reached the cathedral town of Pécs,
A charming town, but the heat us did vex!
Next day we visited the Serbs' Belgrade.
Our pretty guide, Sophia, quite my day made!

At the break of the next day, there awaits
A great sight, the Danube Gorge or Iron Gates.
And King Decebalus's head carved on a cliff,
His glare set in stone in permanent miff.

Veliko Tarnovo on the Yantra
Deserves better than my meagre mantra!
What can match the town of Arbanasi?
Not a thing, except its girls so sassy!

We've come from Amsterdam to the Black Sea
Through lands and places as varied as can be.
Our journey ends at the port of Constanţa
And so must my poem end with this stanza.

Christmas Thoughts

As we celebrate the Son of God's birth
And enter into the season of joy and mirth,
There is something that should give us great pause –
Do we make too much of old Santa Claus?

The shepherds who came to the stable saw
A little baby, and entered with awe.
They had heard the angels singing His praise,
A hymn they'd remember all of their days.

Likewise, the wise men who came from the East,
They found their King, born the least of the least.
A star they had followed for many a day,
'Til their Lord they saw lying in the hay.

Gold they brought, as a present for a King,
Frankincense, for One to Whom angels sing,
Myrrh, to the Son born from the Virgin's womb,
To show His death and three days in the tomb.

Lord, may Your Word in flesh made manifest
Make our hearts welcome Him as their Guest,
That living our lives with and through His grace,
We may be blest one day to see His Face.

Sonnet
Ash Wednesday Thoughts
The Divided Self

Every morning when it becomes light,
There are two men who rise up and fight.
One of them always wants to do what's bad –
He is the one who makes me sad.
The other one wants to do what is right –
Their struggle goes on 'til day turns to night.

This diurnal battle against sin
Is one that on my own, I cannot win.
So, Lord, help me with your heavenly grace,
That I may not stumble in life's long race.
Only this way can I be victorious,
And, after death, see Your Face so glorious!

I trust in You, Lord, God's Anointed,
I know I shall not be disappointed.

Romans VII, 15-25

Thoughts For Ascension Day

O Lord, by what great condescension
You became Man in Your Incarnation!
By Your Death You became Our Salvation,
Which culminated in Your Ascension.

You have not left us in an orphaned state,
From the Throne of Heaven where You abide,
You have sent Your Spirit to be Our Guide
And Our Help on the road to Heaven's gate.

Lord, as we walk along life's winding path,
Often we stray from Your life-giving Way,
So for Your Grace and forgiveness we pray,
Cleanse us then in Your sacramental bath.

Lord, You know we are but vessels of clay,
Grant us Your Mercy at the end of our day.

Sonnet

A Prayer To St Andrew, For St Andrew's Day

O St Andrew, Patron of our country,
May Our Lord grant Scotland His bounty!
O St Andrew, Patron of our city,
Ask Our Lord to look on us with pity!

St Andrew, you were the first called by the Lord,
May He in our hearts be always adored!
Help us in our turn to spread the Good News.
Starting in our old grey town, St Andrews.

St Andrew, you brought the Gospel to the East!
With your help may we reach Heaven's great feast.
Your brother, St Peter, preached in the West,
May church unity be always our quest.

St Andrew, from your place in Heaven above,
Ask Our Lord to shower on Scotland His love!

Sonnet
Day And Night

When the sun's chariot rose in the sky,
I was fast asleep with firmly closed eye.
When I awoke to the still youthful day,
I watched it climb yet higher on its way.

During the brightness of the day
I thought of little, except work and play.
But as the morning became afternoon,
I began to think the day must end soon.

As the sun's globe set in the western sky,
I realised that I too, soon must die,
And yet that death is not an endless night –
By faith I know I'll wake to a new dawn bright.

The Son of Man arose on the third morn –
He gives me hope I too shall be reborn.

Sonnet
The Eye Of Faith

I would like to speak of the optic nerve,
That which the rest of the eye does serve.
Is it not a matter to provoke thought
That the sight giver is our one blind spot?

The Rising of Our Lord is that belief
Which throws our life's landscape into relief.
That which gives light is shrouded in blindness,
Yet is the summit of Divine Kindness.

Lord, if You are not risen, then our faith's in vain,
But I know that indeed You rose again.
Faith is my spiritual optic nerve,
With it as light and guide I shall not swerve.

By following Your Way may I see Your light
And thus be truly blessed in Your sight.

53

Sonnet
The Road Of Life

"It is foolish to fear what cannot be avoided. The safest thing is to fear nothing but God. Conscience overcomes whatever the evil tongue has composed."
   - Inscription on the Calefactory wall, Inchcolm Abbey

The motor of my life is running down,
But is that something that should make me frown?
All earthly things are subject to decay,
Nothing stays the same, that is Nature's way.

So why worry about death or old age?
It's but the turning of another page.
All life on this earth has its own season
And we do not need to know the reason.

Life's race still has some untold laps to run
Before the next life has even begun.
If, by good deeds, wealth above we can store,
Then Peter will greet us at Heaven's door.

So live a good life and then fear not death!
Eternity begins with life's last breath!

The Mountain

As I went up the hill, cool mist drenched me,
Trials and terrors at every turn wrenched me.
As I climbed slowly up the pilgrim hill,
I doubted if I could reach the summit still.

A very long winding way lay ahead,
A path not many climbers find to tread,
But sometimes three men could be glimpsed ahead,
Despite the sky's countenance being of lead.

What if I should lose my way in the dark?
The narrow road seemed to have few stones to mark.
Then my path broke out of the cloud
And I heard My Friend's Voice, and it was loud:

"Foolish man, why did you worry, why fear?
For I was beside you, and always near."

A Sonnet To Time

"Tempora mutantur, nos et mutamur in illis"

What is time but the measurement of change?
If time stood still, nothing could re-arrange.
There'd be no days, months or seasons to name
And everything would always be the same.

As lochs are stocks of water amassing,
So rivers are flows of water passing
Through time and space, as on their way they go.
Without time, there'd be no rivers to flow!

There are those who say that time is a thief
And that its passage brings both joy and grief.
Yet despite its craze for modernity,
Time's but the prelude to eternity.

So God is not "there" or "then" I avow,
God is eternal, and both "here" and "now".

Sonnet

The End Game

When I was young I was just a pawn,
But I was headstrong and I was thrawn.
As I made my way along the chessboard,
I was proud, and not one to be ignored.

I thought I'd be a soldier or a knight
And vanquish my enemies in the fight,
Or, victorious in life's great hassle,
I'd buy and live in some splendid castle.

Perhaps a different path I would search
And make myself a career in the church,
Or climb to the top in some other way
And be the monarch of all I'd survey.

O foolish soul, for the time is near
When God will whisper "end game" in your ear!

Sonnet
The Passion Play, Oberammergau

The people of Oberammergau
In 1633 made a vow,
A vow on which they would not renege,
That if the Lord spared them from the plague,
Every ten years they would make a play
The Lord's Passion and Death to portray.

This vow they have kept in every age,
When their Passion Play they put on stage.
Through it we see how great was God's love,
That He sent His Son from Heaven above
To suffer and redeem us from our sin,
So in Him a new life we could begin.

Now thanks be to God in every way,
For graces received through the Passion Play.

Sonnet
The Way Of Life

As life is a preparation for death,
Lord, may we love You until our last breath.
Help us to live our lives in such a way,
As we would if we knew it were our last day.

We are but pilgrims in a foreign land –
Show us your paths with Your Divine Hand.
May Your Love and Truth be always our guide,
So that from your road, we may not turn aside.

May the Holy Spirit be our lodestar,
Showing us the way on our journey far.
So, like the Wise Men, may we see Your Face
And kneeling adore at Your Throne of Grace.

Lord, help us sinners to follow Your Way,
Then let us see You in the brightness of Your Day.

Sonnet
Reflections On The "Hail Mary"

What a greeting Gabriel gave Mary,
Of which good news, at first she was chary.
She was to be the Mother of Our Lord,
And carry within her the Incarnate Word.

That is why she was chosen from all the rest
And so forever her name will be blest!
For this reason she was preserved from sin,
To be a holy home for Jesus within.

Eve, our first mother, stained us by the Fall.
Mary, Mother of God, Mother of all,
Pray for us now and at the hour of our death,
And be with us when we draw our last breath.

Holy Mary, Mother of Our Saviour,
Through your prayers may we find God's favour!

Glossary

ST ANDREWS LOCAL PLAN
Ding doon   knock down

STOVIES
Stovies   a stew of potato, onions and meat
Reaming forming a froth or foam
Reeking emitting steam, vapour or smoke
Tatties potatoes

TO A LEECH
Pelf riches, money (in a bad sense), ill-gotten gains
Ettling purposing, intending, planning
Gait manner, conduct, fashion
Wad would

Colin McAllister was born in 1942 in Sao Paulo, Brazil but has lived in St Andrews since 1955. He was educated at the Abbey School, Fort Augustus and at St Andrews University where he graduated with MA Honours in Political Economy and Geography. For 28 years he taught Economics and related subjects at Dundee College. He was Captain of the New Golf Club of St Andrews in 1999 and President of St Andrews Burns Club from 2005 to 2007. Golf is his main hobby, but other interests include Scottish history, the Gaelic language, economics and politics, good wine and malt whisky, and foreign travel. He published 'But Does It Scan?' in 2008.